The Life of an
APPLE

Clare Hibbert

www.raintreepublishers.co.uk
Visit our website to find out more information about **Raintree** books.

To order:
 Phone 44 (0) 1865 888112
 Send a fax to 44 (0) 1865 314091
💻 Visit the Raintree Bookshop at **www.raintreepublishers.co.uk** to browse our catalogue and order online.

First published in Great Britain by Raintree, Halley Court, Jordan Hill, Oxford OX2 8EJ, part of Harcourt Education.
Raintree is a registered trademark of Harcourt Education Ltd.

© Harcourt Education Ltd 2004
The moral right of the proprietor has been asserted.

Editorial: Nick Hunter and Catherine Clarke
Design: Michelle Lisseter and Tipani Design
    (www.tipani.co.uk)
Illustration: Tony Jones, Art Construction
Picture Research: Maria Joannou and Elaine Willis
Production: Jonathan Smith

Originated by Dot Gradations Ltd
Printed and bound in China by South China Printing Company

ISBN 1 844 43300 5
08 07 06 05 04
10 9 8 7 6 5 4 3 2 1

British Library Cataloguing in Publication Data
Hibbert, Clare
The Life of an Apple. – (Life Cycles)
571.8'2373
A full catalogue record for this book is available from the British Library.

Acknowledgements
The publishers would like to thank the following for permission to reproduce photographs: Ardea pp. **11** (Bob Gibbons), **19** (Andy Teare), **29**; Corbis pp. **8** (Darrell Gulin), **10** (John Heseltine); FLPA pp. **5** (David Hosking), **9** (Michael Clark), **12** (David Hosking), **14** (Peggy Heard), **15** bottom (Borrell Casals), **18** (R. Wilmshurst), **20** (David Hosking), **22** (W. Broadhurst), **24** (M. Clark), **26** (Tony Hamblin); Garden Matters (Sam North) p. **23**; Holt Studios pp. **13**, **16**, **25**, **27**; Photodisc pp. **4**, **17**, **21**; Wildlife Matters pp. **15** top, **28**.

Cover photograph of ripe red apples on a branch, reproduced with permission of NHPA (T. Kitchin and V. Hurst).

The publishers would like to thank Janet Stott for her assistance in the preparation of this book.

Every effort has been made to contact copyright holders of any material reproduced in this book. Any omissions will be rectified in subsequent printings if notice is given to the publishers.

The paper used to print this book comes from sustainable resources.

Contents

Any words appearing in bold, **like this**, are explained
in the Glossary.

The apple

Apples are **fruits** that grow on apple trees. Most people and some animals love to eat apples. Like all fruits, apples contain seeds. When you cut one open, you can see the seeds in the core of the apple. Each of these seeds could grow into a whole new apple tree, in the right conditions.

An apple is sweet, juicy and delicious to eat. The fruit's seeds are in its core.

The apple tree

The apple tree is a large plant. It is **deciduous**, which means that it loses its leaves each autumn. Each spring is a new beginning. The tree puts out new leaves and starts to develop new fruits.

Growing up

Just as you grow bigger year by year, an apple grows and changes. The different stages of the apple's life make up its **life cycle**. There are many different types of apple, but they all share the same life cycle.

The seasons

Apple trees do not grow in parts of the world that are very hot all the time, or very cold. They grow in places where there are four different seasons: spring, summer, autumn and winter. During each season, the apple is at a different stage of its life cycle.

An apple tree

The apple begins its life as a flower **bud** on a branch of the apple tree. When the flower blooms, it is **pollinated** – **pollen** from another apple flower touches it. Usually, the pollen is carried from flower to flower by busy honey bees. Once the flower has been pollinated, it can start to develop seeds.

Juicy fruit

Over the summer, the plump fruit of the apple grows around the seeds. By the time autumn comes, the apple is ripe. Some apples are picked by people. Others fall to the ground. They might be eaten up by hungry animals or just lie there and rot. Depending on the weather, it can take six months or more for the apple to rot away.

In winter, buds appear on bare branches.

In spring, the flowers open and are pollinated by bees.

Tiny apples swell around the seeds where the flowers were.

By late summer the apples are ripe.

Inside each apple are seeds that could grow into new apple trees.

This diagram shows the **life cycle** of an apple, from bud to **fruit**.

The tree in winter

During winter, the place where the apple tree grows can be cold. There may be chilly winds or rains. Sometimes snow falls. It covers the ground and the tree's branches.

In an apple orchard, the trees are planted in neat rows.

Just resting

All through the cold months, the apple tree rests. There are no leaves on its branches. They all fell off in autumn, when the weather became colder. The tree looks bare and dead but it is only sleeping. It is storing **nutrients** in its trunk for the year ahead. Towards the end of the winter, it starts using this stored energy to build **buds**. Little buds sprout along the branches of the tree.

bud

In late winter, leaf buds appear along the apple tree's branches.

Losing leaves

Leaves may look solid, but they are mostly made of water. They would freeze and then die in the cold winter weather. So the apple tree loses its leaves each autumn. First, it sucks back all the nutrients from them into its trunk. It saves the goodness for next year's leaves.

Bursting buds

Spring is coming! The weather is warming up. Early flowers, such as daffodils and crocuses, start to bloom underneath the apple tree. All the leaf **buds** on the apple tree burst open. At first the leaves are wrinkled. They soon smooth out, and are ready to soak up the spring sunshine.

In spring, the trees are no longer bare. The branches are covered in bright green leaves.

Birds and buds

At the ends of the knobbly branches of the apple tree, there are more fat buds. Inside each bud is a tightly packed flower. Not all of the buds will become flowers, though. Some of the buds are pecked away – they make a tasty meal for hungry birds.

The flower buds are protected by outer petals, which are called sepals.

Making food

The new leaves create food for the tree. They do this by taking in light from the sun, and air. The leaves mix the sunlight and air with water that has come up from the tree's roots. Together, the air, sunlight and water build sugars that feed the whole plant. This way of making food is called photosynthesis.

In flower

In mid-spring, the flower **buds** open. The flowers are also called apple blossom. The centre of each flower looks yellow. This is where the male and female parts of the flower are. Male and female flower parts need to come together to make the seeds that grow into new plants.

Flowers are not only beautiful — they are useful, too. Their job is to make seeds for the tree.

Flower parts

The flower's male parts are called the **stamens**. These carry grains of yellow **pollen**. The **carpel** is the female part. Its tip is called the **stigma**. Inside the carpel are the flower's eggs, which are called **ovules**.

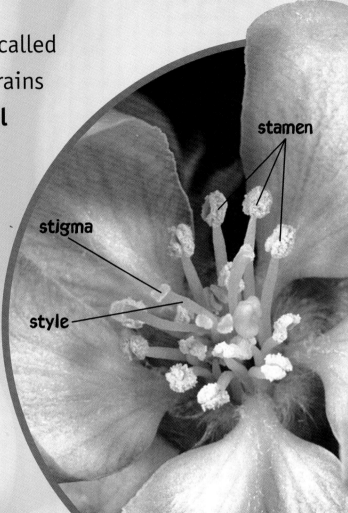

stamen

stigma

style

petal

Family tree

Each flower on the apple tree has pretty white or pink petals. It also has a sweet, rosy **scent**. Apples are related to roses. Their flowers look a lot like wild dog roses.

Busy bee

The flowers on the apple tree contain a sugary juice called **nectar**. Honey bees visit the flowers to collect nectar and **pollen**. The flowers' colour and sweet **scent** attract them.

Pollination

When a bee lands on the flower, grains of pollen stick to its furry body. When the bee visits another flower, sometimes the pollen rubs off on to that flower's **stigma**. This is called **pollination**. The pollen travels down the **style** to the flower's **ovules**. When it joins up with them, seeds can start to grow. This is called **fertilization**.

Bees visit apple tree flowers for sweet drinks of nectar.

Bee-keeping

Most people who keep apple orchards also keep bees. They know that the bees carry pollen from one flower to another. Without the help of the bees, the seeds and **fruit** would not grow.

Bee talk

Most bees in a hive are worker bees. They gather nectar and pollen, which are used to make honey. If a worker bee finds lots of flowers, it rushes back to the hive and performs a special dance. Its movements let the others know exactly where to find the nectar.

Seeds

The flower's job was to attract **pollinating** bees so that it would be able to develop seeds. After pollination, the flower does not need the bees any more. Its petals lose their **scent**. They blow off in the wind and sprinkle on the ground under the tree like snowflakes. The stalks that were holding up the flowers stay on the tree. The seeds will grow inside the stalks. At the end of each one are the sepals – the green outer petals that protected the flower **bud**.

The parts of the flower that are left are the sepals and the ovary. Each ovary is starting to swell into a small apple.

First signs

The part of the stalk just under the sepals is where the flower's **ovary** is. Inside the ovary are the seeds. Over the next few weeks, the ovary starts to swell. It is going to become an apple that will cushion the growing seeds. Its outside wall will be the apple's skin. Its inner wall will be the core around the seeds.

skin

core

seed

This is what the apples will look like when they are fully grown.

Fruit survivors

Soon the tree is covered with bunches of miniature apples. Each one contains up to ten precious seeds. The apples need food and drink from the tree so that they can grow. The tree gives them water, which it has sucked up from the soil with its roots. It also gives them sugars, which it has made with its leaves, using sunlight, air and water. The growing apples use up a lot of water and sugars.

The tree has so many fruits it cannot provide for them all. Some apples drop off when they are still tiny, and are eaten by birds.

Apple drop

After about six weeks, there are too many apples. It is better if the tree only feeds the best ones. Any apples that do not contain many good seeds fall off the tree.

Feeding grubs

Have you ever seen an apple with a tiny tunnel in it? That is where a baby insect, or **grub**, has been eating. Grubs that like to eat into apples include codling moth caterpillars (such as the one in this picture), and apple maggots. They munch the apples even when they are small and sour.

High summer

Throughout the summer each apple keeps getting bigger. The fleshy part of the apple is built of water and sugars. If the weather is very hot and dry, there might not be much water in the ground. People might have to water the apple tree so that the fruits do not shrivel up and die.

Some branches are dragged down by the weight of all the apples.

Bob apple

As well as water and sugar, apples are made of air. This makes them light and able to float. This is useful if they fall off the tree into a stream, or if the land under the tree is flooded when the apples fall. The apples can bob along in the water, away from the tree, taking the seeds to a new place where there is space for them to grow.

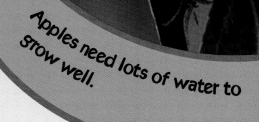

Apples need lots of water to grow well.

Roots

The apple tree has a thick tangle of roots under the soil. They steady the tree so that it won't blow over in the wind. They also suck up rainwater. The water is stored in the tree's trunk. From here, it can go to the leaves or the growing apples.

Ripe and ready

As summer comes to an end, the tree is still covered in leaves. The apple is nearly at the end of its **life cycle**. The tree stops giving it sugars and water. The apple will not grow any bigger, but it still has some changes to make. The seeds need to finish developing. At the moment the apple tastes sharp and sour. It needs to ripen.

These apples are ripe and ready to eat.

Last weeks

Over the next couple of weeks, the apple ripens in the warmth of the autumn sunshine. It starts to smell sweet and attracts hungry, buzzing wasps. Finally, around 22 weeks after the bee **pollinated** the flower, the apple is ready to eat.

Wasps cannot resist a ripe or rotting apple! They nibble holes in the skin to get at the sweet flesh inside.

Skin colour

Apples start out green, but some change to yellow, orange, pink or red as they ripen. Golden Delicious is a type of apple that turns golden yellow. Braeburn apples are a mix of green and rosy red. Granny Smiths usually have a light green, speckled skin. Which colour is your favourite?

Apple harvest

If you have an apple tree in your garden, you and your family will probably eat all the apples you pick. You might share some with your friends and neighbours, too. Some apple **orchards** produce millions of apples. Can you guess where they all go?

Apple picking

No one has invented a machine or robot that is good at picking apples – yet. Apples have to be carefully picked by hand, because they bruise very easily. The pickers use ladders to reach the highest branches.

Apples for sale

Some of the apples are boxed up and sent to shops where people can buy them. Others are pressed. That means they are squeezed very hard to make apple juice or cider. Some of the apples go to factories. They are cooked and used in apple pies, baby foods and other food products.

This enormous machine is an apple press. It squashes the apples so that the juice runs out.

Fallen fruit

Some apples are not picked by people or eaten by animals. They stay on the tree for a while and then drop off. At the same time, the leaves on the apple tree start turning yellow and brown. They, too, fall off the tree, because winter is on the way.

Apple aroma

On the ground, among the fallen leaves, the apples start to go mushy and rot. Their strong smell attracts **fruit**-eating animals.

This squirrel is feasting on a mushy, fallen apple.

Pigeons, thrushes and other birds peck at the fallen apples with their beaks. All sorts of other creatures feast on the soft fruit – from wasps and ants, to mice, rats, squirrels and even deer.

Seed carriers

The way seeds are carried away from the tree is called **seed dispersal**. When animals eat the fruits, they also eat the seeds. Later, when they go to the toilet, they drop the seeds far away from the parent tree. These animal droppings are like ready-made **fertilizer**. Next spring, when the warm weather wakes up the seeds, the **nutrients** from the droppings will help them to grow.

In spring, apple seedlings start to grow. These seedlings will become apple trees one day.

27

New life

Next spring, some of the apple seeds that are resting in the soil might burst into life. This is called **germination**. To germinate, a seed needs warmth and moist soil. It starts to push a shoot up through the soil towards the light. Even if an apple seed does start to grow, it will be a long time before it is a tree that can produce its own **fruits**. The seedling's first shoot will become a stem, and then the stem will thicken out to become a trunk. Every year the tree will grow more and more branches.

This young apple tree is just coming into bloom.

The tree's life

Apple trees start putting out flowers and fruit when they are about eight years old. They can live to be as old as 100! With every single apple the tree makes, the **life cycle** starts all over again.

Short cut

Apple farmers have found a sneaky way to produce new apple trees without seeds. They take a healthy branch from an apple tree and join it on to a plant that is already growing. This is called **grafting**.

This apple tree branch has been cut so it can be grafted (joined) to another tree's branch.

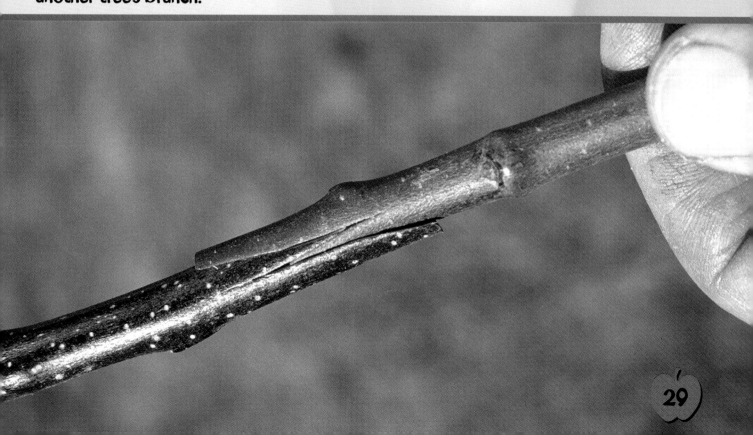

Find out for yourself

The best way to find out more about the **life cycle** of an apple is to watch it happen with your own eyes. Watch your nearest apple tree – or ask an adult to cut open an apple and look inside.

Books to read

I Wonder Why Trees Have Leaves and Other Questions About Plants Andrew Charman (Kingfisher, 1998)
Let's read-and-find-out-science: How do apples grow? Betsy Maestro (HarperPaperbacks, 1992)
Looking at Plants: Flowers, Fruits and Seeds Sally Morgan (Belitha Press, 2002)

Using the Internet

Explore the Internet to find out more about apples. Websites can change, and if some of the links below no longer work, don't worry. Use a search engine, such as www.yahooligans.com, and type in keywords such as 'apple', 'life cycle', 'honey bee' and '**pollinate**'.

Websites

http://www.lecrunch.ie
This website is all about apples, with facts, recipes, fun and games, and much, much more!
http://www.enchantedlearning.com/themes/apple.shtml
Find facts, printouts and activities all to do with apples.
http://www.brainpop.com/science/plantsandanimals/pollination
Play the mini movie to see how flowers are pollinated.

Glossary

bud tightly-packed plant shoot that may open out into a leaf or flower

carpel female part of a flower. It is made up of the stigma, style and ovary.

deciduous tree that sheds all its leaves once a year

fertilization when male and female parts join together to create a new living thing, such as a plant or animal

fertilizer something that is full of the goodness that plants need to grow. Compost and animal droppings are both types of fertilizer.

fruit part of a plant containing the seed or seeds. Fruit is often good to eat.

germination when a seed begins to grow, putting out shoots

grafting taking a shoot or branch from one plant and joining it to another plant

grub young insect that looks nothing like its parent. Adult insects have six legs, whereas grubs usually have none.

life cycle all the different stages in the life of a living thing, such as an animal or plant

nectar sugary food that flowers produce to attract pollinating insects, such as honey bees

nutrients goodness that feeds a plant or animal

orchard garden or field that has been planted with fruit trees

ovary female part of a flower that contains the flower's ovules

ovule female cell, or egg, that can grow into a seed when it has joined together with pollen

pollen powdery grains containing the male cells of a flower

pollination when male pollen from one flower is carried to another flower. This has to happen before a seed can start to grow.

scent smell

seed dispersal carrying seeds to new places where they can grow. Animals help to disperse seeds. So do wind and water.

stamen male part of a flower. Its tip, the anther, carries pollen.

stigma female part of a flower found at the tip of the carpel

style female part of a flower that joins the stigma to the ovary

Index

Titles in the *Life Cycles* series include:

Hardback   1 844 43300 5

Hardback   1 844 43301 3

Hardback   1 844 43302 1

Hardback   1 844 43303 X

Hardback   1 844 43304 8

Hardback   1 844 43305 6

Find out about the other titles in this series on our website www.raintreepublishers.co.uk